Cape Town
an illustrated poem

Julia Grey

First published in 2005 by Struik Publishers
(a division of New Holland Publishing (South Africa) (Pty) Ltd)
New Holland Publishing is a member of Johnnic Communications Ltd
Log on to our photographic website www.imagesofafrica.co.za
First edition. Second print.

Garfield House, 86-88 Edgware Road, London W2 2EA, United Kingdom, www.newhollandpublishers.com

80 McKenzie Street, Cape Town 8001, South Africa, www.struik.co.za

14 Aquatic Drive, Frenchs Forest, NSW 2086, Australia

218 Lake Road, Northcote, Auckland, New Zealand

ISBN 1 77007 189 X

10 9 8 7 6 5 4 3 2 1

Publishing manager: Dominique le Roux
Managing editor: Lesley Hay-Whitton
Editor: Erika Bornman
DTP: Sian Marshall
Photographer of original artwork: Paul Sutton, Hirt & Carter

Reproduction by Hirt &: Carter Cape (Pty) Ltd
Printed and bound by Craft Print International Limited

play
maharani

Contents

1
2
3
4
5
6
7
8
9
10
11
12
13
14
15
16
17
18
19
20
21
22
23
24
25
26
27
28
29
30
31
32
33
34
35
36
37
38
39
40
41

MADE IN SOUTH AFRICA

is book is dedicated to

my parents: John and Janet Grey

my brother: Matthew and his wife – Lisa [nee Collier]

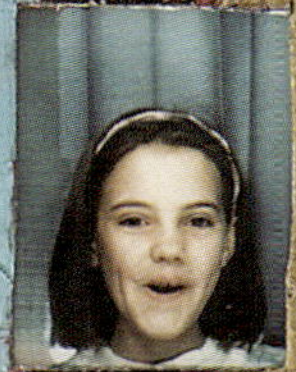

my grandparents: Bill and Mary Basson [nee Wiley]

Joyce Grey [nee Congdon]

Jacob Aikman

Ruth Scott

Andrew Jamieson

Lungile Ludidi

Sebastiaan Soeters

today tastes like a pretzel, we climb up lion's head
close our eyes to the sun for the world
to turn red
then we twist our bodies to shape as a tree
disappear into cape town's bucklebent knee

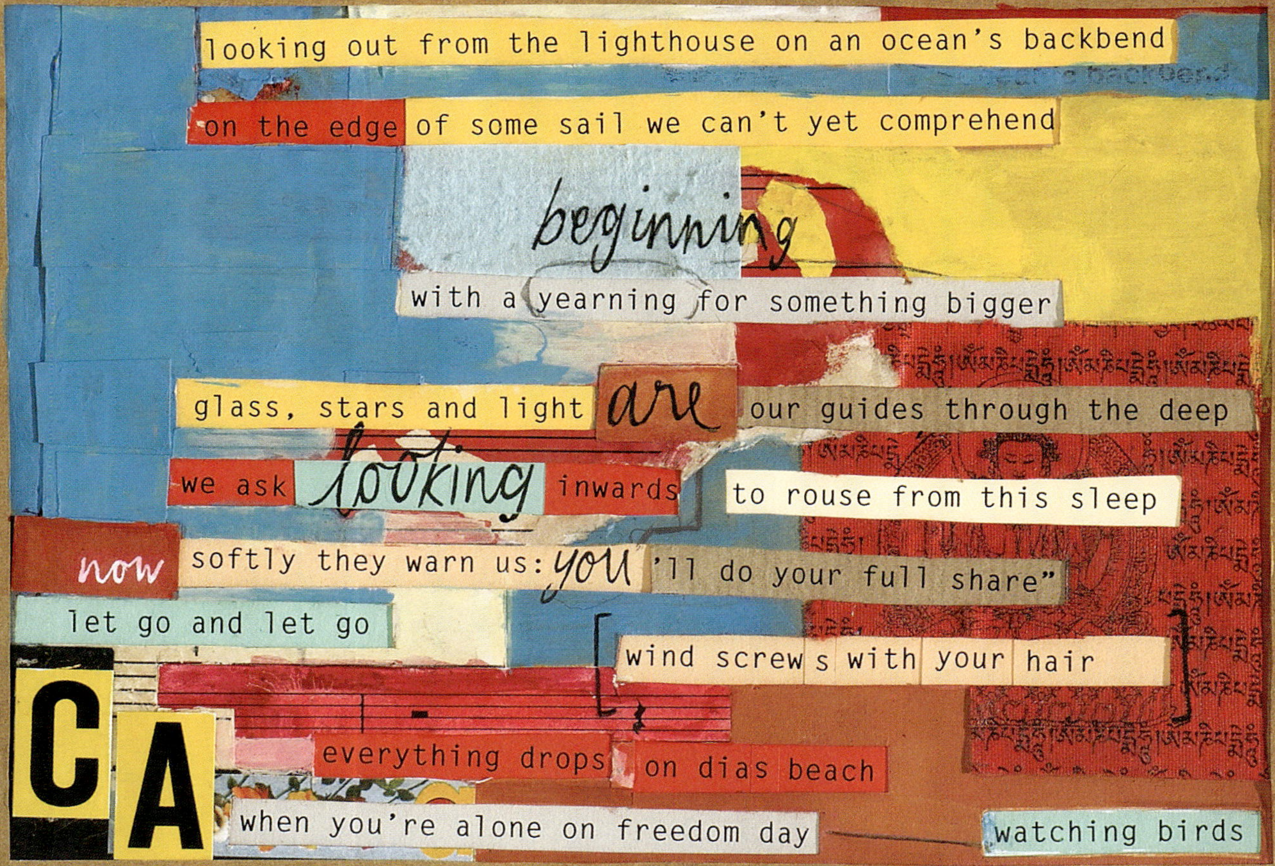
looking out from the lighthouse on an ocean's backbend
on the edge of some sail we can't yet comprehend
beginning
with a yearning for something bigger
glass, stars and light are our guides through the deep
we ask looking inwards to rouse from this sleep
now softly they warn us: you 'll do your full share"
let go and let go
wind screw s with your hair
C A
everything drops on dias beach
when you're alone on freedom day
watching birds

Peninsula
w Pages
ROBERTSONS
THE SPICE PEOPLE
Rajah
CURRY POWDER
A unique blend of the finest spices
MILD & SPICY
CAPE
PO
INT
Groendam
Cape Maclear
Platbank
Plumpudding Rock
ce on straight
C12-3
Taco
C12-4
Nacho
C12-5
Quesadilla

there is a lookout point on the road to red hill
where jah has been painted in black
on a white wall. down below, ships lie like toys
waiting to play
first they must harness the south-easter
"out of the harbour now,
face the storm free
learn about waves
on an open heart sea"

Simon's Town
Long Beach
Simonsbaai
Cole's Point
North Peak
Simonsberg
MINERAL WORLD

play.
create.
wet sand is for drip towers
dry sand is for spit pancakes
look up for the train
and see instead, a little woman in a
yellow
raincoat
she scuffles alone along the boardwalk
holding
one of those little plastic windmills
attached to a straw
it leading her
like a floating candle on open water
Muizenberg
Kalkbaai
Vishoek
Glencairn
Simon's Town
Miller's Point
Smitswinkelbaai
Da Gama Monument 1497
Cape of Good Hope
Cape Point

KALKBAAI-BERG
Kalk Bay
Trappies
Fish Hoek
Vishoekbaai
Jager's Walk
Cove
M 4
Quarry Rock
Glencairn
Elsebaai
Shelley
fish hoek

fishermen that respect her darkness,
may harvest from the sea
Something's there in the water below your dangling feet
kelp in ocean swell the last lone infidel
singing in the subway
on your way to the brass bell
PANCAKE KAYA
and there you are. amidst saturday,
slap chips and beer
looking through the water
for the subtle thing behind it

KaLkBAy
POST CARD.
FOR CORRESPONDENCE
ONLY THE ADDRESS TO BE WRITTEN HERE
KB36AT
KALKY'S
FISH & CHIPS
PIZZERIA

broken green bottles
lie between railway tracks
then tumble and humble
into (community)
rock pool

ST JAMES
No. 1340

FINE
FOODS
THE FEAR OF JOY 111
We must bring up
children to rejoice in good and beautiful things, but
not through fear of retribution and punishment of hell.
We must love Goodness because it is good, and be-
cause we wish to represent a higher type of man.
ear to the ground
something is stirring
it will shoot through
the soil
like that bump
on boyes drive
on the mountain, a phoenix
fine-feathered and wise
looking firewards and trusting
he flies

MUIZENBERG
EMPIRE CAFE
he children if
he life aims
aims. And
his strongest power
ver," erects before
blime aim in life, so
world, and so uplifting
of life is . . . to be
ybody has somewhat
which allures him so
so far, to a measure
diminish the dis
ish dream bit by bit to a cruel
TOLL ROUTE
TOLROETE
religion
existence of
vision and a more emotional
es become gradua
our emotions b
lous to suffering a
cruelty, and
life is warped by t
much preoccupation with cold,
realities. Fortunately,
134

outside the alphen spar, a bird made its nest
in a robot that covered the red light in jest
then there was the man on brommersvlei road
who strode in the sun through the plants of a nursery
(sucking one of those lollipops
they give to the kids)
he walked as though amongst untamed forest
the birds eating from his fingers

Constantia

a platform safe
against the skirt of a mountain patterned
with birds, berries and guitars
on the other side of the river is a man cutting reeds
those are the same
baskets he has been
making for the
last twenty-three years
only now, a little less tidy
and a little more blind
(dignity could be a man weaving in a suit)

Kirstenbosch

flasks stars blankets at a maynardville show
looking for magic. trees lit at the back - exciting green hue
creative possibility just waiting for glue
[what role. script. costume.]
could you be a little nihilist; it's tenfold more vibe
(pity your soul can't be shaken aside)
could you be a little trendy, it might help to belong
which trendoid is spinning
SPIRIT
YOU ARE ONE
your exact song
CAMERAS
Kodak
FILM

tasara
Date
Datum
MAYNARD-VILLE
THEATRE / -TEATER
MAYNARDVILLE
OPEN AIR THEATRE
BUTLER'S PIZZA!
FREE DELIVERY
wynber

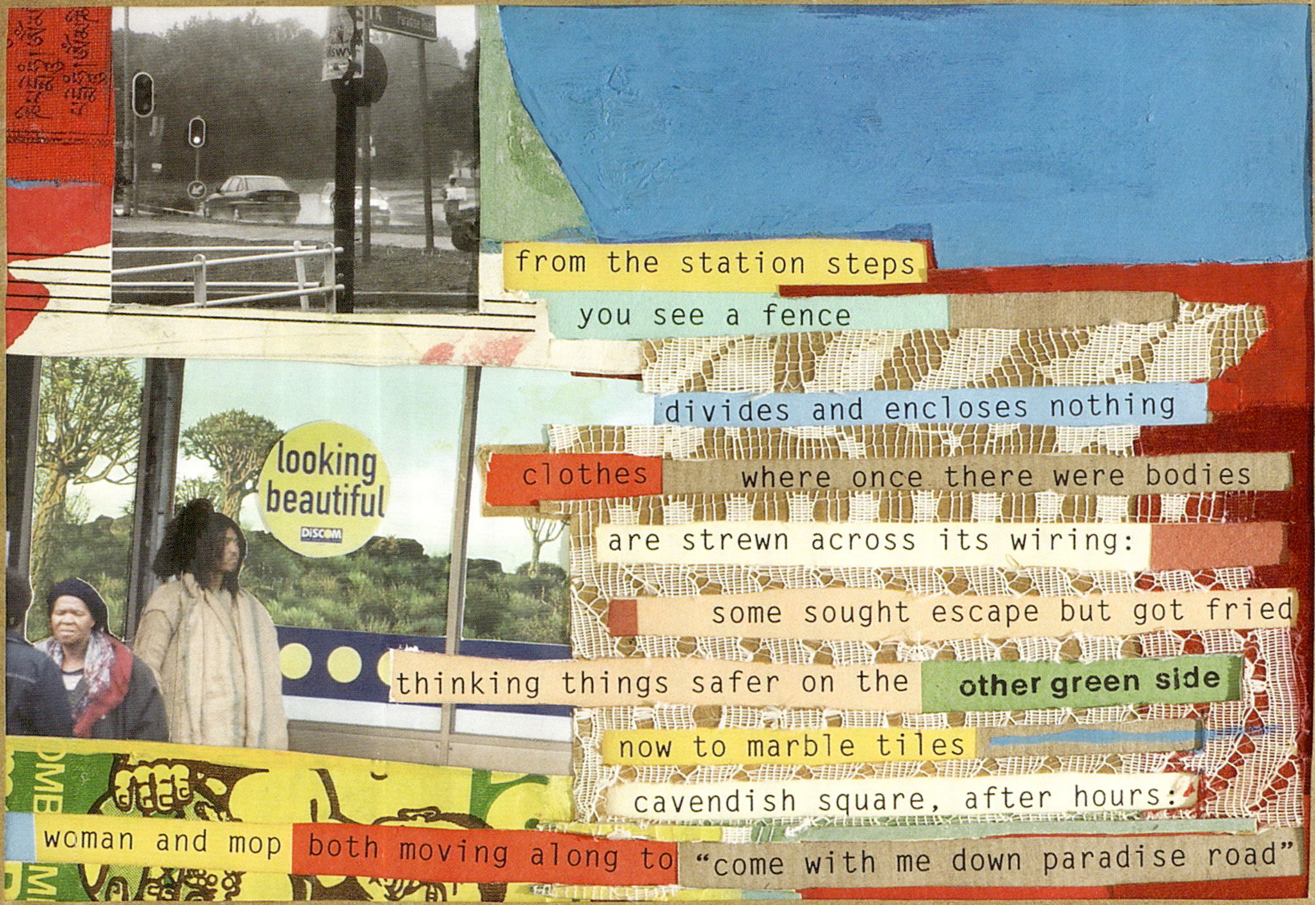
looking beautiful
DISCOM
from the station steps
you see a fence
divides and encloses nothing
clothes where once there were bodies
are strewn across its wiring:
some sought escape but got fried
thinking things safer on the other green side
now to marble tiles
cavendish square, after hours:
woman and mop both moving along to "come with me down paradise road"

SCULPTURED RUGS
CAPE TOWN
Claremont

boerewors roll
seat with a view
south africa - australia
twenty-six; twenty-two
MAY 1995 KICK OFF
SOUTH AFRICA
disinterested in all of that
is a boy who sits below
the railway bridge
carefully decanting the dregs
Audi Centr
from discarded drink
bottles

W. P.
NEWLANDS

ideas
whether yours, someone else's
or my own
with apologies to someone
these ideas
have felt like **stone**
every so often
we had to sit by the
dam
ENERGY

university of cape town
TABLE MOUNTAIN
EASTERN TABLE
Fir Tree
Grotto Caves
Echo Valley
Orions Cave
Waaikoppie
Hiddingh Buttress
Ascension
3030
3060
JUNCTION PEAK
Hely Hutchinson
Woodhead
Ranger
Fernwood Buttress
Window Buttress
The Aloes
Reserve Peak
2770
Scout Club Hut
Nursery Buttress
Victoria
Wynberg Caves
Diamond Spring Path
Ranger
2483
Klaassens Kop
Kloof
KIRSTENBOSCH
National Botanical Gardens
Tea Room
NEWLANDS MUNICIPAL FOREST
Woodstock Cave
Plum Pudding Hill
Kings Blockhouse
Mowbray Ridge
Rhodes Memorial
Eastern Buttress
University
Reservoirs
SPES BONA
Mowbray
Rosebank
Rondebosch
Newlands
Claremont
WYNBERG HILL
640
Kenilworth

cry into mussel soup at café matisse
sit
with the ache til you feel it release
moving in cycles:
women
dandelions
coffee shops on rondebosch main road
where once
you could read with wine at any hour
hoping the right conversation
would walk in
ERDIE SEËL GEB
N INHOUD NA V
ANGS ERKEN WO
RUSTENBURG
Tony's
Campground
Supermarket
Coca-Cola
B

RITE
Bank
RIVERSIDE MALL
Rondebosch

i want the feeling to touch rockbottom
said a guy
at touch of madness
drinking peppermint tea
go look
for someone conscious
to look into us and say
“you already know
deep down
it’s always okay”
SAFETY MATCHES
10 BOXES

SAFETY MATCHES
LION
10 BOXES
10 DOSIES
MATCHES•VUURHOUTJIES
INDEPENDENT
ARMCHAIR
THEATRE
OBZ CAFE
DOMINION
HARDWARE STORE
123
OBS

walls
where peeling paint reveals
a history of colour
laid upon colour
in don pedro's, the tables are
arranged perfectly
(close together)
A TO Z
2ND HAND STORE

woodstock
Fairweather
CLASSIC PANEL SHOP
PLAZA
RoopKiRani
Don Pedro
Restaurant
Coca-Cola
M & S Parker

zuma resounds from the earth's core
a seashore
where plastic-trumpet seals
(dreadlocked, smoking weed)
are positioned well away from any uptight creed.
unskinned peanuts and a box of chockstix
"not here for soccer, just for the chicks"
R KING
सुगंधी
TRADE
MARK
REGISTERED
पुष्प गुच्छ
G. BY :- SHAH AGARBATTI & CO. MADE IN INDIA
68 KALYAN STREET. DANA BUNDER.BOMBAY.9

EN PYNAPPELS
UITVOERKWALITEIT.
PRODUK VAN REPUBLIEK VAN S.A.
ATHLONE
STADIUM
Sugar
Sugar
Computicket
Computicket
frica vs Jamaica
Stadium
Apr 2003

cape town: child
once psychologically screwed
in the formative years
by her fat father's rude
sense of design
and she's pushed
to stop crying
"pull yourself together"
there are long hours of therapy
she still has to
weather

Langa

PER LUGPOS
BY AIRMAIL
PAR AVION
nationalism:
loose answer to this need to belong
a mindset (getting it wrong)
left us isolated from cultural sharing
an african upbringing
a place to get bearing
(my passport's not european although i'm of that descent)
a world with less boundary is what
we think
was once meant
freedom a soul that can move
love choosing to stick
with the good thing you found
BY AIR MAIL
par avion
CAUTION
Tie with string

cape town international

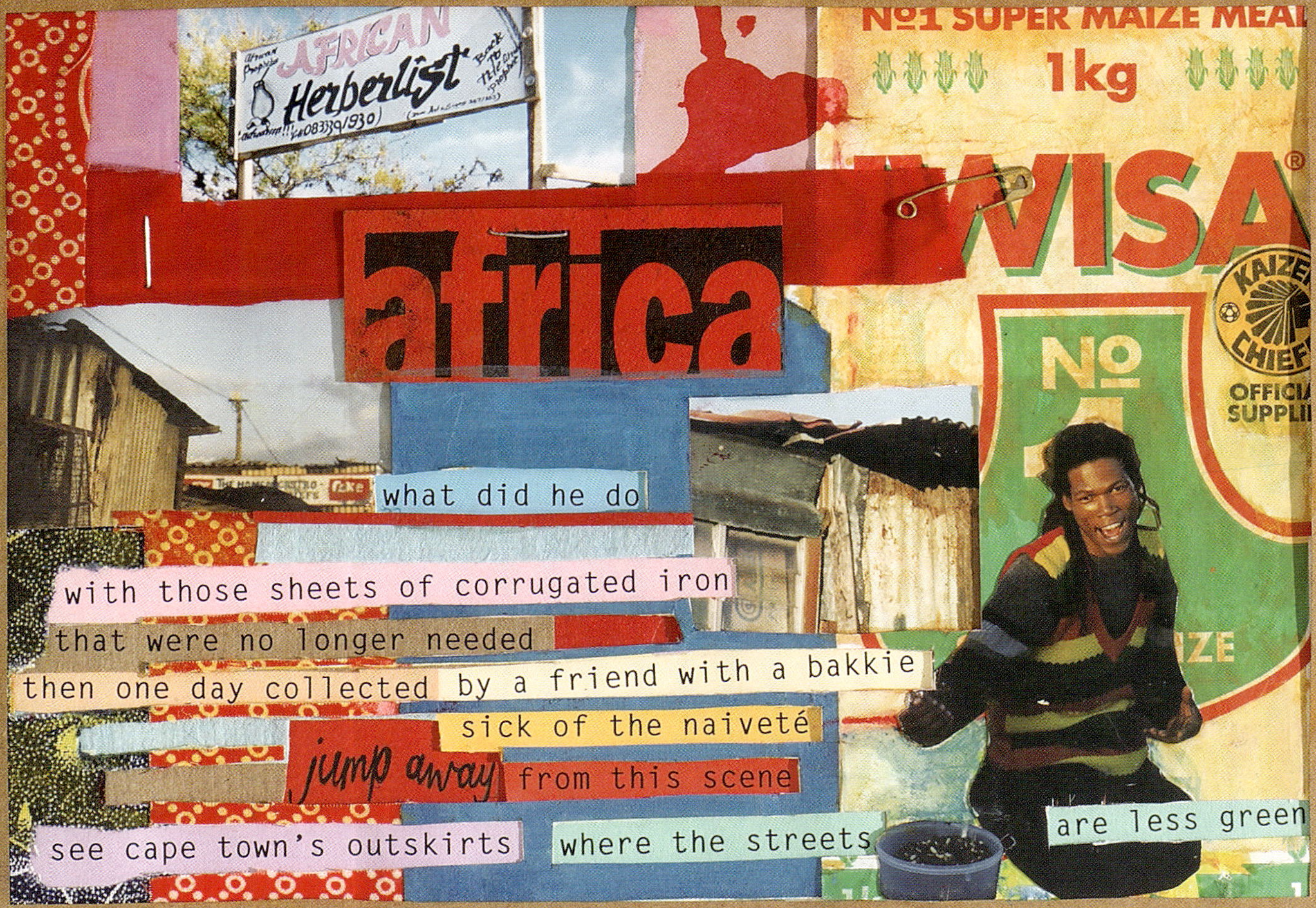
AFRICAN
Herberlist
No1 SUPER MAIZE MEAL
1kg
WISA
africa
No
KAIZER CHIEFS
OFFICIAL SUPPLI
what did he do
with those sheets of corrugated iron
that were no longer needed
then one day collected by a friend with a bakkie
sick of the naiveté
jump away from this scene
see cape town's outskirts where the streets are less green

AMASI
ESELWA™
KHAYELITSHA
MITCHELLS PLAIN
Kh a yelitsha

today the rain
sounds like one thousand people
breaking open pistachio nuts
an abnormally big star
was also spotted
it looks like another messiah
might just be born
ten kilometres away
on some cape flats "lawn"
we are standing here chasing
something for a moment,
forgetting it's already ours
the core

BLOUBERG
Circus Ninja.
EMAGIN.
I CRIED THE OTHER DAY BECAUSE A GIRL HELD MY HAND.

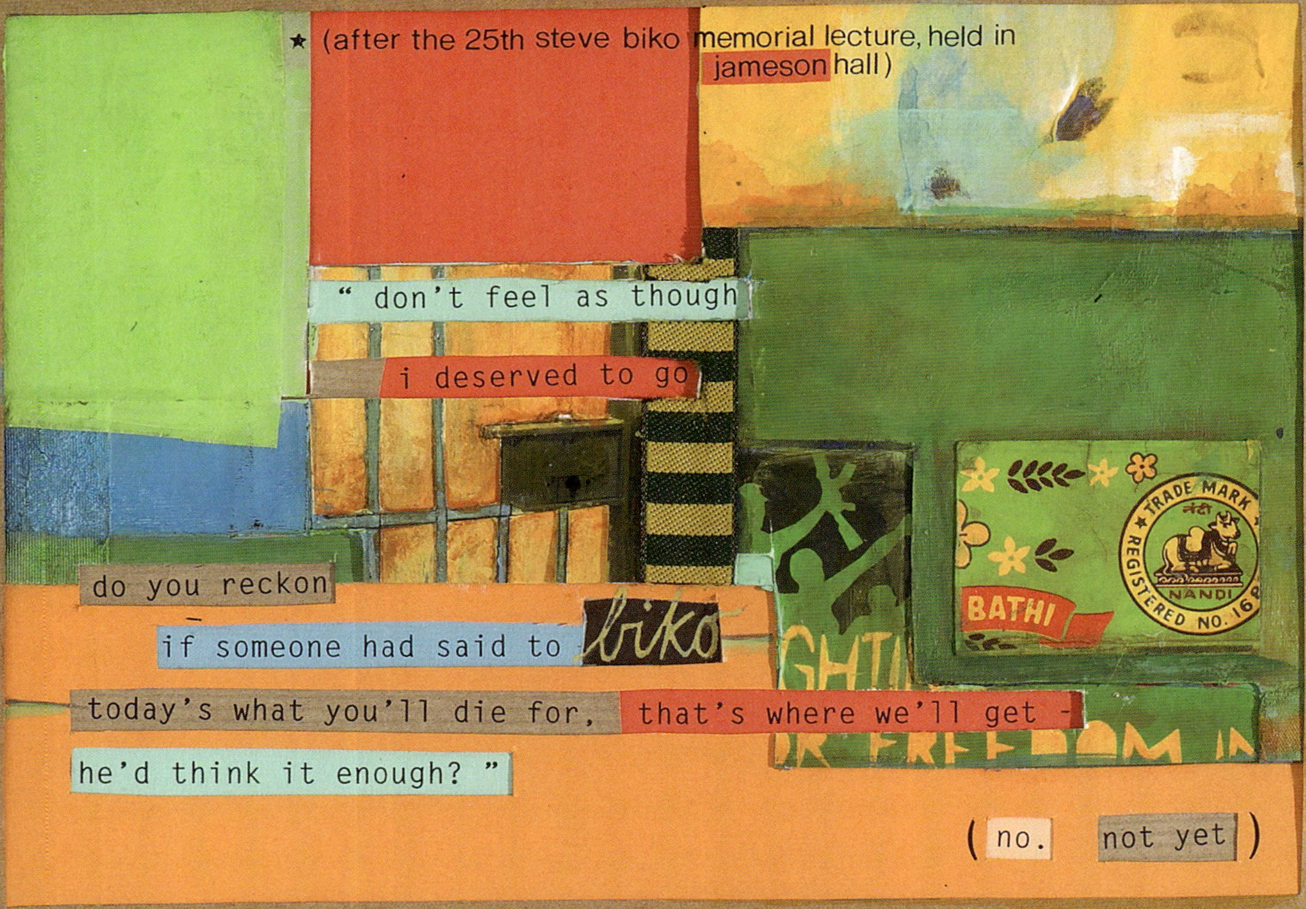
* (after the 25th steve biko memorial lecture, held in jameson hall)
" don't feel as though
i deserved to go
do you reckon
if someone had said to biko
today's what you'll die for, that's where we'll get -
he'd think it enough? "
(no. not yet)
BATHI

Robben Island
June 1964 along with Nelson Mandela, Walter Sisulu, Ahmed Kathrada and others in the 'Rivonia Trial'. He was charged under the Sabotage and Suppression of Communism Acts with attempting to overthrow the government by violent revolution and by assisting the armed invasion of the country by foreign troops. The charge sheet listed 193 acts of
persons recruited by the accused in their capacity as members of the High Command of MK
No details known.
He is on Robben Island.
In 1970 Mbeki obtained an honours degree in economics through ... prison. In 1978 he was awarded an honorary doctorate by the University Amsterdam in Holland.
Mbeki is married with three sons and one daughter
Mbeki was convicted and sentenced to life imprisonment on Robben Island.
Mbeki was tried in the Pretoria Supreme Court from October 1963 to
ore being brought to court Mkwayi had been detained in solitary confine- for months, and subjected to torture. Those who saw him at his trial ed that he was unrecognisable.
No details known.
He is on Robben Island.
He is on Robben Island.
the State of Emergency
aba has eight children. His wife died while he was in prison.
soned for life.
he is serving on Robben Island.
ing the trial Mkwayi told the court that, like his leader Nelson Mandela, s prepared to die for his 'ideal of a democratic and free society in which sons live together in harmony and with equal opportunities'.
tion with this trial, Joseph Mdluli, died in security police custody in March 1976 as a result of 'force applied to his neck' according to the post mort
He is married with childre
He is married
aid he was 'injured while trying to escape'
No details known. He is on Robben Island.
No details known. He is on Robben Island.
etails known. He is on Robben Island.
He and his wife have one child
He is married with
He is married with child
He is married with two daugh
trial one of the accused said that statements d made before a ate had been dictated by the police.
Johnson Mlambo was branch chairman of the PAC in
l study priveleges were removed from him and
in solitary confinement for a year.
After the sentence the nine men stood up in the dock, gave the clenched fist ANC salute and sang 'Nkosi Sikelele Afrika' and were joined in the singing by spectators.
Mokoape said that over the years they had spoken out against the humiliation of the pass laws, the agony of migratory labour, the horror of innocent children dying of starvation and the scars inflicted by incidents such as Sharpeville and Langa and no-one had disputed the truth of what they said.
etoria 12' trial was widely described as the most important political trial ace in South Africa since the Rivonia trial of 1963/64. During the
was a security policeman. He admitted being a former member of the PAC from which he had deserted to the ANC
sentence was passed Ramotse raised his fist in an ANC salute.
Ramotse was a member of the ANC before it was banned. He was first arrested in Johannesburg in 1961 following explosions in Port Elizabeth.
si was convicted and sentenced on 14 February 1977 to 16 years' imprisonment which he is serving on Robben Island.
ourt Nkosi was described as a witch doctor and was said to have been the who incited others to arson. In his statement Nkosi claimed that he was to enlist young people in a black power movement.
At the trial one of the accused said that statements they made before a trate had been dictated by the police.
Nkabinde suffered from pleurisy on Robben Island, and no treatment was given to him for more than three years.
He was taken to a Rhodesian prison and there 'stripped naked, beaten and given electric shocks and chained naked to a cell floor'. South African police arrived and joined in the assaults upon him. He was then taken to Pretoria where he was again tortured. The security police took him back to Rhodesia for helicopter flights over Zambia and Rhodesia to point out 'certain things'. After this he was taken back to South Africa, where he was repeatedly tortured until his trial.
ring the trial one of the accused told the court that when he was arrested as questioned by three sergeants, one of whom hit him when he denied ledge of arson. He was told to take off his clothes and was bound with rags. as then told to sit on his haunches, a stick was placed under his knees and en his elbows. He was made to hang on the stick between tables. He said: thing was used to bite my back, buttocks and private parts'. A medical confirmed that four of the five accused had marks on their bodies.
During his trial Matthews told the court that his actions had been motivated by a desire to make a better South Africa for his children to live in. Although he had grounds for appeal against sentence, he refused, saying that he was proud to be sentenced along with his co-accused.
Matthews was a bookkeeper

welcome to our city
pretty as a postcard
here we have our mountain.
here we have our sea.
we have covered filthy dockyard
- scrubbed it,
made it pretty
we are planning an express line
that'll link it to site b
The Bindi People
CAPE TOWN
Durban

QUAY FOUR
MFULENI
SITE C
TAIWAN
Nolungile
Nonqubela
GREEN POINT
SITE B
KHAYELITSHA
GRIFFITHS MXENGE
EASTRIDGE
WATERFRONT

pain is a barren scar on the mountain slope
wounds need to be given time
we are growing
even if not apparent on the outside
let the ground lie fallow
ear to the earth

District Six
1960's
2004
ZONNEBLOEM

her back is a mountain
her arms cradle
she knows
we need extra nurturing
during transition

city bowl

City of Cape
LAUGH IT OFF
we knew no better
some of us
upon arrival,
built forts and castles
now we are studying these structures
to find appropriate means of protection
walls
no longer necessary
AIDS
SHOUT THE ODDS, BARK DISSENT.
BECOME A CULTURE JAMMER
www.laughitoff.co.za
We call on all workers, unemployed, students and youth to build Anti-War Committees and join us in a
MARCH TO PARLIAMENT
SAT. 5 APRIL '03 @ 10am
KEIZERGRACHT STR
District 6 (Opp Castle)
Free trains from 8am - wear a red armband or ribbon.
Phone: 447 6777 / 073 155 5529 / 082 456 1631
rubber south of this line

arving hysterical naked
the castle
Mouille Point
Green Point Common
Green Point.
Sea Point
SIGNAL HILL
Lions Rump
Culemborg
THE CASTLE
Tamboers Kloof
LIONS HEAD
Clifton
No bananas south of this line
THICK AND
Creamy
Real Dairy
AMASI
Roses
INCENSE

berg wind on the parade
people buy fastfood lunches;
earbuds; dolls; nighties
cellphone covers
and dry bunches
of buchu
on a beer crate is a card game
slowdancing to what sounds
like frank sinatra
or preaching
(sound distorts when it is booming
from a speaker)
"put your trust in jesus"
or just panties and paprika

GRAND PARADE

as a kid lying lengthways: car's textured backseat
on the christmas-lights drive back from adderley street
look up back to front
to see an angel's reflection
(in the dark, bodies know the instinctive direction
of a vehicle bound homewards) lampposts overhead
tracing treetops for bearings til you're carried to bed
3c
3c
DIRECT IMPORTER OF
Jewellery, Watches,
MARBLE AND OTHER
CLOCKS,
STREET, CAPE TOWN.

Adderley street

she wants to straddle

the way all good gateways should.

kenya and
congo.

are cornered in cape town

(what will it take for us to remember)

africa's not just drumming on djembe

greenmarket square

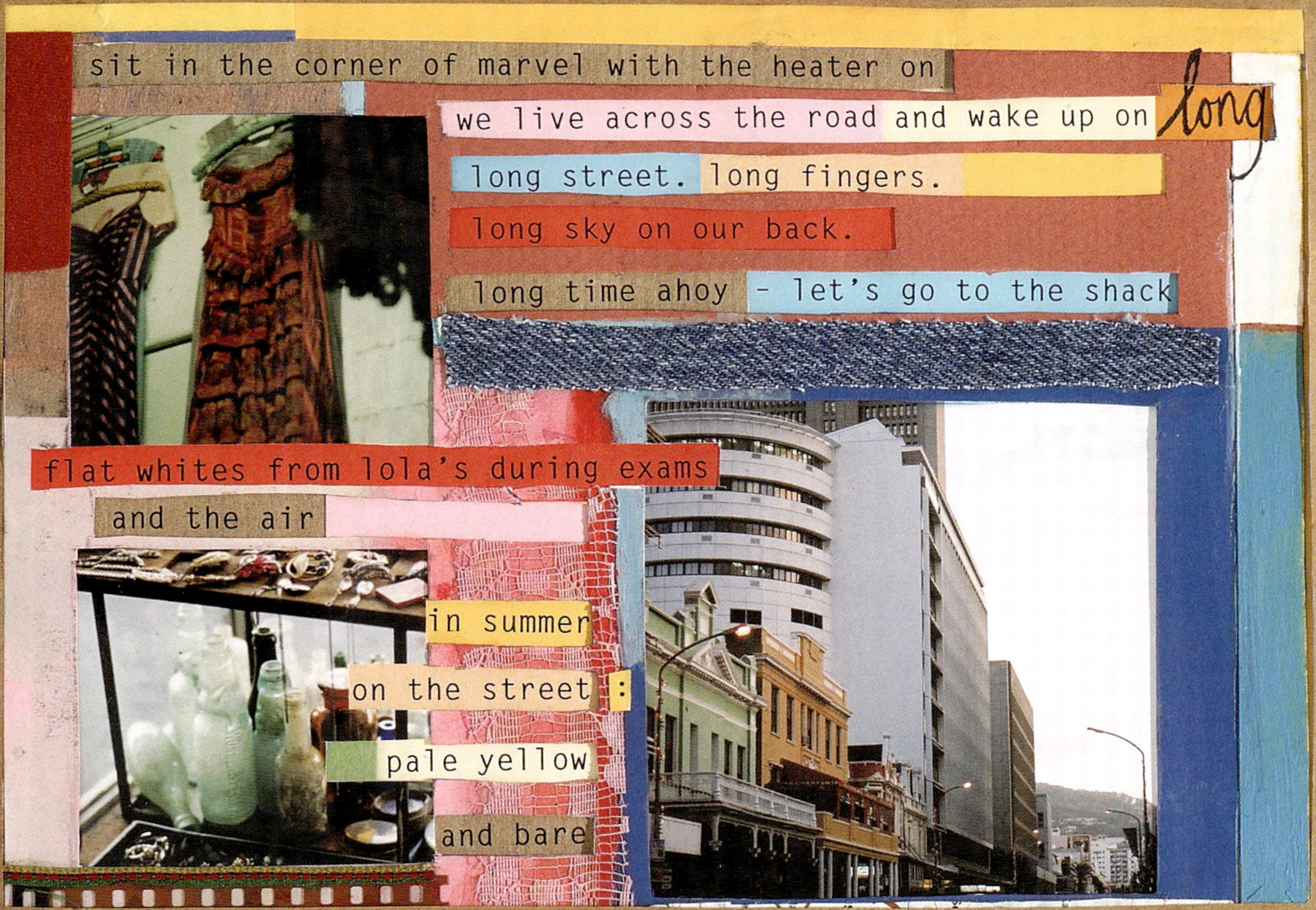
sit in the corner of marvel with the heater on
we live across the road and wake up on long
long street. long fingers.
long sky on our back.
long time ahoy - let's go to the shack
flat whites from lola's during exams
and the air
in summer
on the street :
pale yellow
and bare

MAMA
AFRICA
R. PICKWICKS
Jo'burg
long street

jasmine arrives at conversation between
people that grapple with this need to be seen.
here we are, making musical instruments
“ keep looking down
hammer away ”
in a gardens park at
twilight,
rain falls on a man
he is drenched
and playing a pennywhistle

Saigon
VIETNAMESE
RESTAURANT
MIMMO'S
OPEN
OPEN
Standard Bank
AutoBank
KLOOF STREET

a.m.
victoria court
from up the road,
a mosque calls
samoosas from uncle allie's
ice-cream coloured walls
veiling could also be:
woman's free right to hide
shut out the rest
go swimming inside

Rose Corner
CAFE
16
bo-kaap

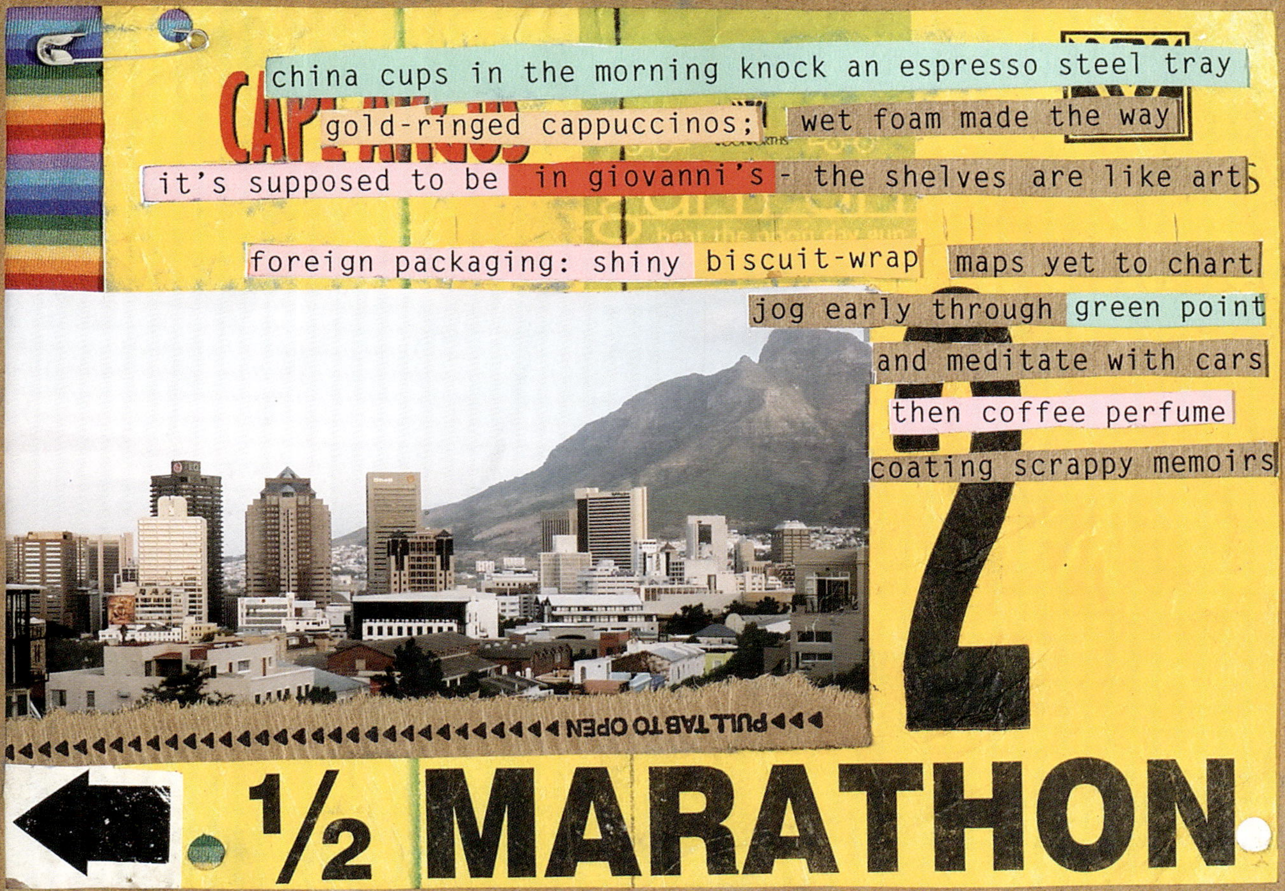
china cups in the morning knock an espresso steel tray
gold-ringed cappuccinos; wet foam made the way
it's supposed to be in giovanni's - the shelves are like art
foreign packaging: shiny biscuit-wrap maps yet to chart
jog early through green point
and meditate with cars
then coffee perfume
coating scrappy memoirs
PULL TAB TO OPEN
½ MARATHON

GREENPOINT
55
55

twilight on ocean view drive
where the sea and sky settle into oxidised metal
and lapis lazuli
(looking for magic through windows)
500 g
woman in a kitchen
WHEN PACKED
her watch catching
light
snake
ng mixture
one floor below :
a man shining
MTOMB
silver
BLEND

sea point
New
Chicke
Schwarm
ONLY 16
KING
DISEASE
BB
Smoking mixture
BEST BLEND
BEST BLEND TOBACCO (PTY) LTD
SUNRISE
HARD TOFFEES
SAFETY MATCHES
10 BOXES
LIO

sea
2
sky
and twelve knights
at her back

Test your stain remedy on a hidden seam or hem.
Soak items for at least one hour, preferably overnight.
F TON
Kasteels Buttress
Wood Buttress
2584
RIZLA+
KING SIZE
MEDIUM WEIGHT ROLLING PAPERS
THE WORLD'S FAVOURITE
PECK'S
ANCHOVETTE

never been classy chicks
tried in high school with the private school cliques
clothes, mediocrity looking
for a man
trying to look hot with copious
fake tan
dress up at sixteen,
mom drops you at blues
perfectly white linen;
uncomfortably high shoes
hopefully we'll settle on a different
mentality
posh places are mostly
too much a formality
Save Tibet

CAMPS
BAY
it" pattern, ou w
We've included th

there is a window (a portal) as the sun hits the skyline
from this rock on llandudno, distant bodies become shadow
it's
like that scene from that movie
where they're all facing east
taking communion on surfboards
with a setting-sun priest
POST + CARD
in a cathedral of
mountain
moon (stained-glassed and above)
souls paddling out
homewards
to infinity.
blue. love
"Chic" Series. Charles Worcester & Co., Bristol

on straight grain of fabric
A
Simplicity
5554
SIZE 16
SHIRT FRONT
Devant du chemisier
Frente de la blusa
Dart – Fold along solid line. Stitch along broken line.
Geelkip Buttress
Myburghs Corner
LLANDUDNO

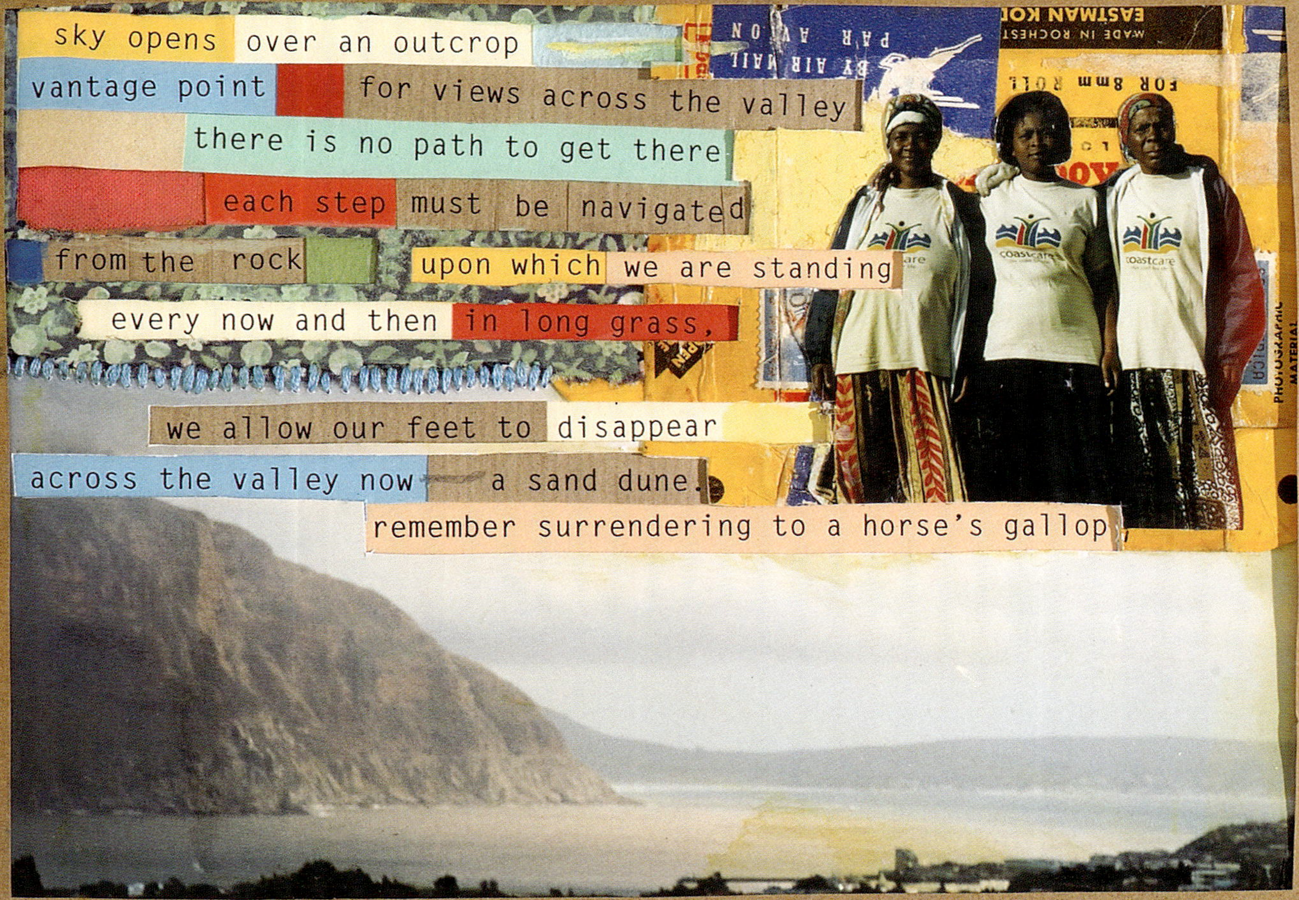
sky opens over an outcrop
vantage point for views across the valley
there is no path to get there
each step must be navigated
from the rock upon which we are standing
every now and then in long grass,
we allow our feet to disappear
across the valley now a sand dune.
remember surrendering to a horse's gallop

A13-6
Nectar
A13-5
Sun Gold
A13-4
Mystic Maize
CK
Kodachrome
PILCHARD
4615
WIDTH
5,5mm
Hou
T
CAMERAS
bay

between our head and our heart, there has been a road
under construction for lifetimes.
now they are joining just like lines on our palm
our heart may be sore but our centre is
calm
we sailed east
and found zen
transcendental clear mind
engen onestop til
emotions aligned

chapman's peak
Milieu du devant
Centre Front
Seam line
E
Simplicity 5554

on noordhoek beach,
a ship lies tattered,
on the long walk
towards its skeleton,
you notice your footprints.
they have become measured

ART FARM
THE · RED · HERRING
TRADING · POST
WELCOME · PLEASE DRIVE IN
NOORDHOEK
Sandy Bay
Houtbaai
Duikerpunt
Noordhoek
Chapman's Bay
Kakapo 1900
Kommetjie
Slangkoppunt
Clan Monroe 1905
The Island

we know where the rocks lie
- lighthouses
have shown
we navigate more safely
as we
head back for home

Kommetjie

looking out from a rock
on an ocean's
backbend
the edge of one sail that has
come
to an end

scarborough

when things are going badly,
we climb up lion's head
close our eyes to the sun
for the world to turn red
then we twist our bodies to shape as a tree
and disappear into cape town's bucklebent knee
aradis

Roger Hudson; Tammy Lancaster; Frances Trahar; Colwyn Thomas; Katie Spiegel; Alistair Moulton-Black; Lulu Beyers; Amy Cornfield; Julia Merrett; Claire Homewood; Kate Muller; Kirsten Colquhoun; Karl Penzhorn; Luke Hutchinson; James Bisset; John Duncan; Tristyn von Berg; Adam and Firle Davies; Mariella Furrer; All the boys at Elukhuselweni, Khayelitsha; the Phakamisa crew; Carly Tanur, Clinton Osborne and Brian Kilbey; Brian Little; Doreen Scott; Henry and Nadine Aikman; Lynn Groll; Jean Wheeler; Jeffrey Rink; Gus Ferguson; Malcolm Payne; Jane Young; Joanne Friedlander; Diane Awerbuck; Ian Reed (Umfolozi); Sherelene Michaels; Guy Westmoreland; Vivian McLean; Carol Marsh; my late uncle John Basson; Luan Anderson; my great-great-grandmother Mary Nightingle; Alan and Clemency Grey; Tuan and Dilys Marais; Alanis Morissette; Dave Matthews; Alistair's Mom's friends at Findhorn; Rustenburg Girls' Art Department; The School of Practical Philosophy; Dominique le Roux, Erika Bornman, Sian Marshall and Lesley Hay-Whitton at Struik;

www.greenteabag.co.za; Laugh It Off; Corné and Twakkie; flat 58 Priory Heights (Rog, Boris, Rich); Andrew Aikman; Thabo; Patricia Gebers; my first art teacher Mrs Beckley; Dan Eldon; Sabrina Ward Harrison. The person who left details of Political prisoners in a Michaelis printer.

Photo credits

Dedications page: Ruth by Philippa Coleman; Andy by Claire Thomas; Lungile by Carly Tanur and Seb by Mikhael Subotsky Cape Point: Africa map by Colwyn Thomas. Muizenberg: Scarred veld and Empire Theatre by Jake Aikman. Kirstenbosch: Freshly-ground photos by Julia Merrett. Claremont: Looking beautiful and Paradise Motors by Seb Soeters. Khayelitsha: Top right-hand corner by Colwyn Thomas. Blouberg: Burnt cones by Jake Aikman. Llandudno: Luke surfing by Shannon Armour. Hout Bay: Landscape shot from bay by Seb Soeters. Chapman's Peak: Sea view by Andy Jamieson. Scarborough: Julia by Jake Aikman.

love